AQUARIUM

HOW JEANNETTE POWER INVENTED AQUARIUMS TO OBSERVE MARINE LIFE

Written by Darcy Pattison & Illustrated by Peter Willis

Moments in Science

Mims House Books
1309 Broadway, Little Rock, AR 72202

Text copyright © 2023 by Darcy Pattison
Illustrations copyright © 2023 by Mims House
All rights reserved.

MimsHouseBooks.com

Publisher's Cataloging-in-Publication data

Names: Pattison, Darcy, author. | Willis, Peter, illustrator.
Title: Aquarium : how Jeannette Power invented aquariums to observe marine life / written by Darcy Pattison; illustrated by Peter Willis.
Description: Includes bibliographical references. | Little Rock, AR: Mims House, 2023. | Summary: In 1818, Jeannette Power, a young French woman, invented the aquarium so she could observe the argonaut octopus.
Identifiers: LCCN: 2023901807 | ISBN: 978-1-62944-232-7 (hardcover) | 978-1-62944-233-4 (paperback) | 978-1-62944-234-1 (ebook) | 978-1-62944-235-8 (audio)
Subjects: LCSH Villepreux-Power, Jeanne, 1794-1871--Juvenile literature. | Aquariums--France--History--19th century--Juvenile literature. | Women marine scientists--Biography--Juvenile literature. | Women marine biologists--Biography--Juvenile literature. | Marine scientists--Biography--Juvenile literature. | Marine biologists--Biography--Juvenile literature. | Octopuses--Juvenile literature. | BISAC JUVENILE NONFICTION / Animals / Marine Life | JUVENILE NONFICTION / Biography & Autobiography / Science & Technology | JUVENILE NONFICTION / Biography & Autobiography / Women | JUVENILE NONFICTION / People & Places / Europe | JUVENILE NONFICTION / Science & Nature / History of Science
Classification: LCC QH91.3.V55 2023 | DDC 578.77092--dc23

In 1818,

Jeannette leaned on the ship's rail, watching the waves. The young French woman was sailing to the island of Sicily to marry her fiancé. It was the first time that she had sailed the Mediterranean Sea, and the waters captivated her.

Soon Jeannette was tramping across Sicily,

studying its plants, animals, and fossils. But always she came back to the sea. On clear, sunny days, she could watch the marine animals swimming next to her boat.

Oceanography and marine biology were difficult sciences in the 1800s because there was no way to observe live animals at close range for long periods of time.

Most humans can only hold their breath underwater for about two or three minutes. That's not long enough for good observations. Most studies of marine animals were from dead creatures that had been caught in fishing nets.

Jeannette wanted to study marine animals while they were alive.

She asked fishermen to save unusual catches in barrels of seawater, an easy cage for live animals. At the day's end, she sorted through the barrels and bought the plants or animals that interested her. But once animals were out of their habitat, the ocean, it was hard to keep them alive for long.

Small or dainty

marine life was difficult to see in the barrels. Instead, Jeannette gave the fishermen glass vases with cork lids. That allowed her to easily study snails and other small marine life.

In 1832,

Jeannette started to study a 4-inch (10 cm) long octopus, the *Argonauta argo*. Most octopuses live on the ocean floor, but this one lived in the open sea, often near the surface. And it always had two of its eight arms tucked into a furrowed shell about 8 inches (20 cm) wide.

Scientists argued about the *Argonauta argo*'s shell. Most scientists thought that the octopus just found an empty shell, like a hermit crab. However, a few scientists thought the octopus made its own shell.

Jeannette needed a way to study live animals over time. Observation was the only way to solve the mystery of the octopus's shell.

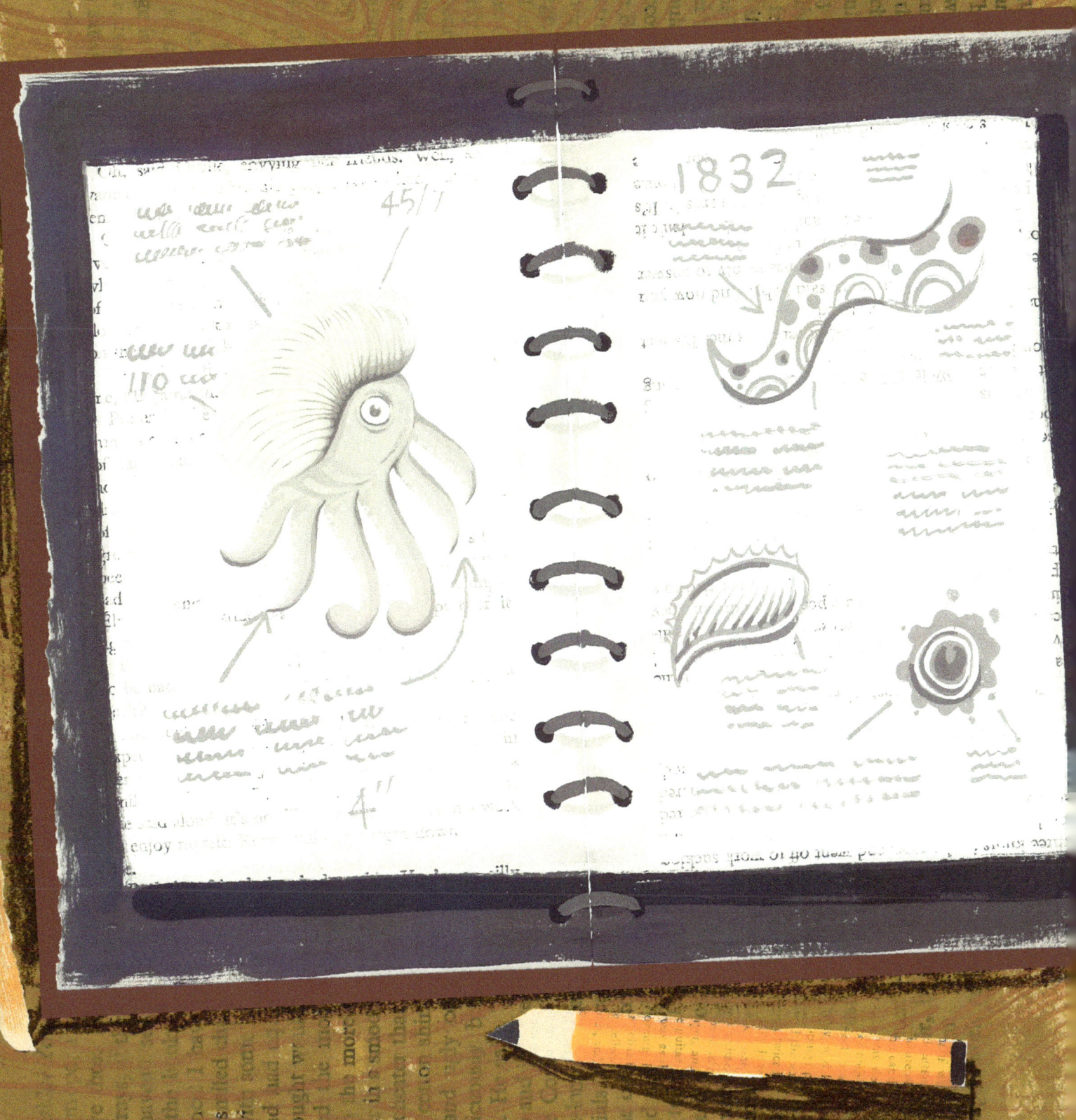

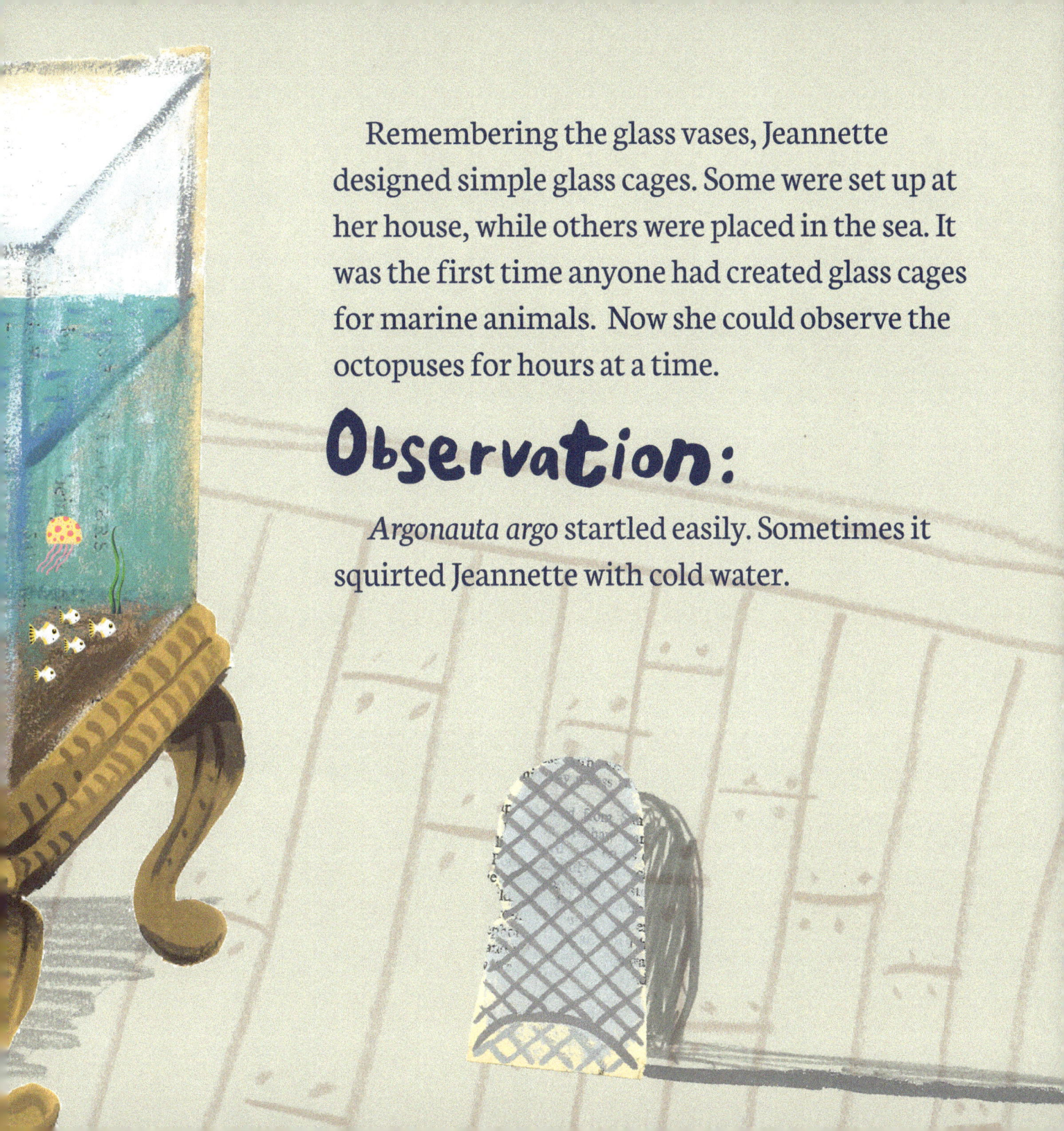

Remembering the glass vases, Jeannette designed simple glass cages. Some were set up at her house, while others were placed in the sea. It was the first time anyone had created glass cages for marine animals. Now she could observe the octopuses for hours at a time.

Observation:

Argonauta argo startled easily. Sometimes it squirted Jeannette with cold water.

The glass cages at her house weren't perfect, because after a day or two the water became stale.

The water had to be changed or the sea creatures died. Keeping the sea creatures alive was hard!

Because the port of Messina, Sicily, had clear water, Jeannette also built wooden cages that she had anchored in the sea. Here, the water was always fresh. Between the glass and wooden cages, either at her house or in the sea, Jeannette spent hours each day observing the octopuses.

Observation:

Jeannette described *Argonauta argo*'s arms, body, and shell in detail. Like other octopuses, this creature had eight arms, each with suckers. Two arms were always within the shell. The two arms farthest from the shell were longer. They had suckers but ended with unusual circular paddles. Some stories said that the octopus used these paddle arms as sails. But no one really knew why the arms were paddled.

Because her octopuses lived in cages, Jeannette had to feed them.

Some days, Jeannette sailed with the fishermen and used nets to catch the kind of food the octopuses usually ate. Other days, fishermen stopped by with buckets of their day's catch to see if she wanted to buy anything.

Jeannette patiently watched the octopuses, day after day, specimen after specimen. Over a 10-year period, she estimated that she had observed over 1,000 individual octopuses.

Observation:

Jeannette described how *Argonauta argo* hunted and ate. The octopuses ate plankton or used their arms to capture small fishes. Sometimes they rode on a jellyfish while feeding on it. Jeannette often hand-fed her octopuses. Only once did an octopus tear a finger with its beak.

Observation:

Argonauta argo's shell looked delicate, but Jeannette had never seen a broken one.

To prove that *Argonauta argo* made its own shell,

Jeannette needed to observe this happening. She broke one octopus's shell and put the octopus back into the cage. She also added other broken *Argonauta argo* shells.

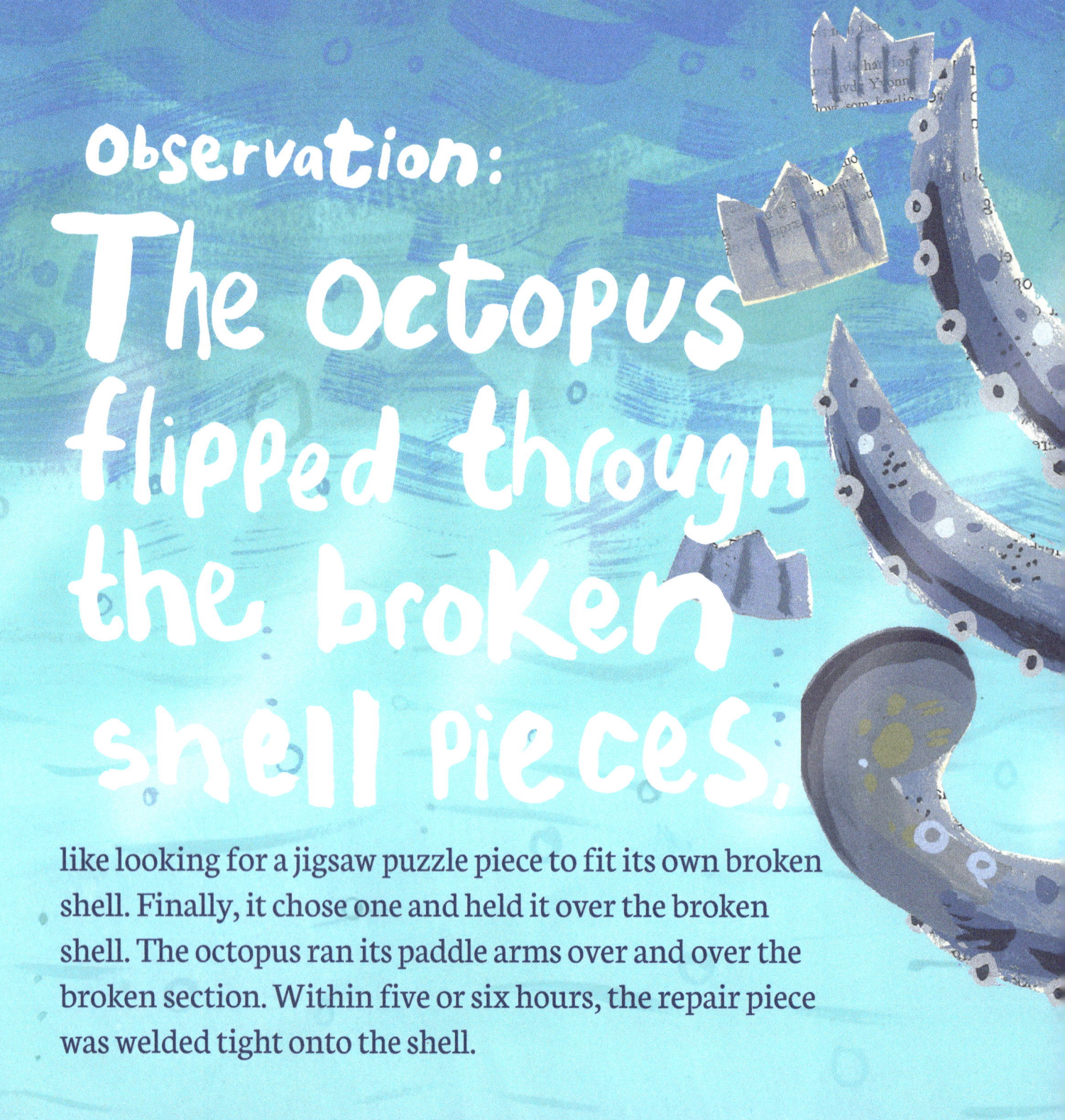

Observation:
The octopus flipped through the broken shell pieces,

like looking for a jigsaw puzzle piece to fit its own broken shell. Finally, it chose one and held it over the broken shell. The octopus ran its paddle arms over and over the broken section. Within five or six hours, the repair piece was welded tight onto the shell.

Conclusion:

Jeannette's patience in observing the octopus over time allowed her to solve a scientific mystery.

Jeannette had discovered that *Argonauta argo*'s paddle arms made the shells. Her glass and wooden cages allowed her to observe the process as it happened.

Before Jeannette's glass and wooden cages—

now called aquariums—oceanography and marine biology were difficult. The aquariums, however, allowed humans to observe live sea creatures. Now others could be captivated by the sea and its creatures. Just like Jeannette.

THE WORLD'S WEIRDEST OCTOPUS - *Argonauta argo*

Often called a paper nautilus, the *Argonaua argo* octopus lives in tropical or temperate seas around the world. Like all octopuses, the *Argonauta argo* has eight arms, but the female has two special arms. These arms are larger and paddle-shaped. They secrete calcium carbonate, which the octopus uses to build her own shell. Most octopuses live on the ocean floor, but the *Argonauga argo* lives in the open sea. The shell holds air to help the female octopus float. This bouyancy helps the octopus to move through the water.

The shell also acts as a place to shelter newborn octopuses. Females can grow up to 5inches (13 cm) long, and their shells can be up to 12 inches (30 cm) long. Males are much smaller than the females, less than 1 one inch (2 cm) long. To mate, the male detaches an arm that carries his sperm and leaves it inside the female's shell. Newborn female octopuses start to grow their own shells at about 12 days old.

Female *Argonauta Argo* shell. Image public domain.

POWER CAGES - The First Aquariums

Glass cages that could keep marine animals alive transformed the study of marine life. For the first time, scientists had a controlled aquatic environment to observe animals from at all stages of life. Aquariums also allowed scientists to exhibit rare and beautiful marine and fresh-water animals to an interested public.

Jeannette Power invented three types of aquariums. Small glass cages could be set up at her home. If her house was near the ocean, pumps circulated ocean water through hoses to keep the water fresh. Other glass cages were set inside wooden boxes and then placed into the ocean. Here, the animals had fresh water and food, so they stay alive longer.

Finally, for larger specimens, she built wooden cages that were anchored to the ocean's floor. Each type of cage or aquarium was used for different observations of marine animals. In Jeannette's honor, the Gioenia Academy and the Zoological Society of London named these aquariums cages à la Power, or Power cages.

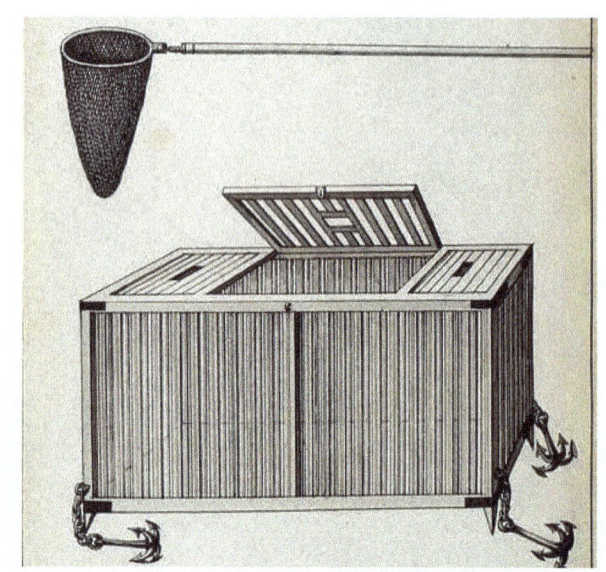

JEANNETTE VILLEPREUX POWER (1794–1871)

Jeannette Villepreux Power was born in Juillac, France, in 1794. At the age of 17, she traveled to Paris to work as a seamstress. She quickly became an expert at embroidery, and in 1816 she was asked to work on the wedding dress of Sicilian princess Maria Carolina. Because of the royal wedding dress, she met James Power, a wealthy merchant. They were married in Messina, Sicily in 1818, and they lived there for 25 years, before returning to France.

While in Sicily, Jeannette studied the plants, animals, and fossils of the island. She wrote two guidebooks about Sicily. She adopted a pair of martens (a type of weasel) and put a tree in her house for them to climb and sleep in. Often, however, the martens chose to sleep in Jeannette's bed. She found an active scientific community on the island, with many who specialized in marine animals. With their encouragement, she began her study of the *Argonauta argo*. Her first scientific papers were presented to the Italian scientific community. However, Jeannette also wanted them read by the French scientists. At a friend's urging she sent a copy of her research to Mr. Rang, a marine scientist. Unfortunately, he used her research and claimed that he had done observation and experiments with the *Argonauta argo*.

British biologist Richard Owen, known for coining the term Dinosauria, encouraged Jeannette and helped her assert that she was the inventor of the aquarium. He presented her work to the Zoological Society of London, and she was elected a member in 1839. It was just one of many recognitions for her work.

In 1838, Jeannette sent some of her specimen cabinets and papers to France, but the ship sank, and most of her work was lost at sea. James and Jeannette moved back to France in 1842, where she died in 1871.

Besides studying the *Argonauta argo*, Jeannette also studied meteorites, as well as butterflies and their caterpillars. In 1997, a crater on Venus discovered by the Magellan probe was given the name Villepreaux-Power in her honor.

Disdéri, André Adolphe Eugène (1861), photograph, Musée d'Orsay, Paris. Photograph of Jeanne Villepreux-Power.

"I did not study this marine animal…using the imagination, but by experimental observations." — Jeannette Power

OCEANOGRAPHY – Underwater Study

Water covers over 70% of Earth. And yet, because humans can't breathe water, the study of the oceans and their marine life has been hard. Here's a timeline of inventions that have helped people stay underwater longer.

c. 375 B.C.: Diving Bell. Aristotle reported that the ancient Greeks used a diving bell, which is a water-tight container set upside down in the water to keep the air inside. Swimmers could come up into the diving bell to breathe, and then dive down again.

1535: Diving Bell. Italian Guglielmo de Lorena designed a diving bell that was small enough to be worn by a man. Using slings to hold the bell in place, a swimmer could carry his air with him.

1620: Underwater Vessels. Dutch inventor Cornelis Drebbel designed the first underwater vessel. Submersibles are underwater vehicles that rely on air support, usually through a hose, from the surface or from compressed tanks of air. Submarines are also underwater vehicles, but they are fully contained and don't rely on surface support.

1829: Diving Suits. British inventors Charles and John Deane designed a diving suit with a hard helmet. Hoses from the surface pumped air to the suit.

1942: SCUBA equipment. Frenchman Jacques-Yves Cousteau co-designed the first scuba gear, which gave divers a compact way to carry breathing air with them. Scuba is an acronym for self-contained underwater breathing apparatus.

1962: Underwater Habitat. Belgian Robert Sténuit became the first aquanaut by spending over 24 hours at a depth of 200 feet (61 meters) in an underwater habitat, a structure designed by American inventor Edwin Link, for people to live in underwater.

SOURCES

Association Jeanne Villepreux-Power. http://jeanne-villepreux-power.org/

D'Angelo, Michela. "From 'Cinderella' to 'Lady of the Argonauts': Jeannette Villepreux Power in Messina (1818-1843)." Sicilian Naturalist, series 4, vol. 36 (2), (2012): 191-224. Translated by Google. https://www.academia.edu/23719947/da_cenerentola_a_dama_degli_argonauti_jeannette_villepreux_power_a_messina_1818-1843

Power J. 1842. Continuazione delle osservazioni sul polpo dell'Argonauta argo, fatte ne' mesi di ottobre, novembre, e dicembre del 1839. [Continuation of observations on the octopus Argonauta argo, made in October, November, and December 1839.] http://www.fundacionmuseo.org.ar/wp-content/uploads/The-role-of-female-cephalopod-researchers-Suppl.pdf Cited PDF p. 34

Experiments and Observations on the Argonauta argo. By Madame Jeannette Power. Communicated by Professor Owen, F.R.S. Report of the Fourteenth Meeting of the British Association for the Advancement of Science, held at York in September 1844, Notices and abstracts of communications, pp. 74-77.

Power J. 1857. Observations on the habits of various marine animals. Annals and Magazine of Natural History (second series), XX: 334-336.

VIDEO OF THE ARGONAUTA ARGO: Nguyen, Dam. Paper nautilus sighting off California. https://youtu.be/0-4JYPXPSrk

Milton Keynes UK
Ingram Content Group UK Ltd.
UKHW051840040823
426284UK00003B/41